Unpitched Aural

Specimen tests for Drum Kit

for Trinity College London exams

Grades 1-8

Published by
Trinity College London
www.trinitycollege.com

Registered in the England
Company no. 02683033
Charity no. 1014792

Printed in England by Halstan & Co. Ltd, Amersham, Bucks.

Introduction

This book aims to help teachers prepare their students for the unpitched aural section of Trinity drum kit exams. It contains specimen examples of the four tests given for each grade.

The four tests given for each grade are designed to develop the candidate's abilities in the fields of musical perception, discrimination, memory understanding and analysis. The tests are carefully graded from application of basic skills to more advanced understanding. In the actual exam, Parts 1, 2 and 3 of this test will be administered using a CD (where a specialist examiner is not present)*; Part 4 will be administered live.

Part 1   Time Signature

The candidate will be asked to recognise the time signature from a rhythmic phrase played twice on the snare drum. The phrase will use one of the time signatures associated with the grade taken, as indicated in the cumulative table on page 3. The pulse will be given and accents placed on the first beat of the bar.

Part 2   Style Recognition

The candidate will be asked to recognise the musical style of a pattern played on the drum kit. The style will be taken from the cumulative grid on page 3.

Part 3   Identify the Changes

The candidate will listen to a short piece played twice/three times on the drum kit. On the second playing the examiner will introduce one or more changes. The changes will be to *either* the rhythm (rhythmic change) *and/or* the drums/cymbals played (pattern change). The pattern change may be either a change to the order in which the drum(s)/cymbal(s) are played or the introduction of a different drum/cymbal.

From Grade 3 onwards the examiner will give the candidate a printed score of the original version of the piece. The candidate will be expected to respond as outlined in the table on page 3.

Part 4   Playalong

The examiner will play a short piece of music twice on the piano. The candidate will be asked to listen to the piece on the first playing. On the second playing, the candidate should accompany the examiner on the drum kit using appropriate style, rhythm and fills for the grade taken. The time signature and count-in will be provided by the examiner before the second playing. At Grades 1-4 the examiner will state the style; for Grades 5-8 the candidate will be expected to recognise the style. The styles used will be appropriate for the grade based on the styles list given in Part 2 (see page 3). Recordings of these tests are available to download from www.trinitycollege.com/percussion

Contents

* In specialist centres in the UK all parts will be administered live, though the candidate will have no visual line to the drum kit.

Grade requirements

Grade	Part 1 Time Signature (cumulative*)	Part 2 Style Recognition (cumulative*)	Part 3 Identify the Changes	
			Change(s)	Required response
1	$\frac{2}{4}$ $\frac{3}{4}$ $\frac{4}{4}$	Straight 8s feel ✓ Basic Latin feel ✓ $\frac{3}{4}$ Straight ✓	1 change: rhythm *or* pattern	Raise hand to identify moment of change
2	$\frac{6}{8}$	$\frac{12}{8}$ feel ✓ Basic $\frac{2}{4}$ March ✓	1 change: rhythm *or* pattern	Identify the type of change
3		Basic Rhumba ✓ Indie Rock ✓	1 change: rhythm *or* pattern	Identify the bar in which the change occurred
4	$\frac{12}{8}$ $\frac{9}{8}$	Bossa Nova ✓ Shuffle ✓ Show 2 feel ✓ Reggae ✓	1 change: rhythm *or* pattern	Identify the bar in which the change occurred *and* the type of change
5	$\frac{5}{4}$	Swing ✓ Jazz Waltz ✓ Tango ✓ Disco ✓	2 separate changes: 1 of rhythm *and* 1 of pattern	Identify the bars in which the changes occurred *and* the type of change
6	Any	Funk ✓ Samba ✓ $\frac{6}{8}$ Afro Cuban ✓	2 changes involving: rhythm *or* pattern *or* rhythm and pattern	Identify the bars in which the changes occurred *and* the type of change
7		Mambo ✓	3 changes involving: rhythm *or* pattern *or* rhythm and pattern	Identify the bars in which the changes occurred giving a detailed explanation of the nature of the change
8		New Orleans 2nd Line ✓	3 changes involving: rhythm *or* pattern *or* rhythm and pattern	Identify the bars in which the changes occurred giving a detailed explanation of the nature of the change

* Please note, at any given grade candidates are expected to know the requirements of the preceding grade(s).

Grade 1

Part 1   Time Signature

The examiner will play a rhythmic phrase twice on the snare drum in a time signature appropriate to the grade (see page 3). The pulse will be given and accents placed on the first beat of the bar. The candidate will be asked to identify the time signature.

Example 1

Example 2

Example 3

Part 2   Style Recognition

The examiner will play a short piece twice on the drum kit in a particular musical style appropriate to the grade (see page 3). The candidate will be asked to identify the style.

Example 1 – Straight 8s feel

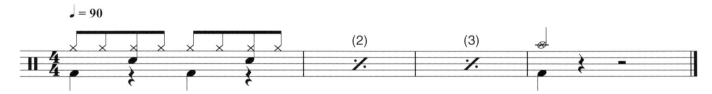

Example 2 – Basic Latin feel

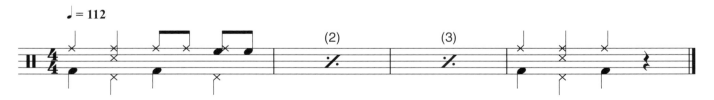

Example 3 – ¾ Straight

Part 3   Identify the Changes

The examiner will play a short piece twice on the drum kit. On the second playing a change will be introduced to *either* the rhythm (rhythm change) *or* the drums/cymbals played (pattern change). The candidate will be asked to raise their hand to identify the moment of change.

Example 1
original version

a) changed version – rhythm change

b) changed version – pattern change

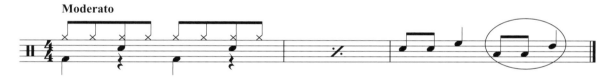

Example 2
original version

a) changed version – rhythm change

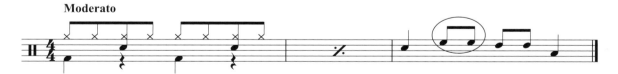

b) changed version – pattern change

Example 3
original version

a) changed version – rhythm change

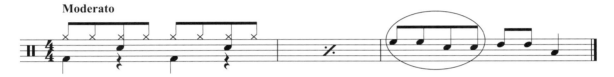

b) changed version – pattern change

Part 4   Playalong

The examiner will play a melody twice on the piano. On the second playing, the candidate will be asked to accompany the examiner on the drum kit using appropriate style, rhythm and fills. The style, time signature and a count-in will be given before the second playing.

Example 1 – Straight 8s feel

Example 2 – Straight 8s feel

Example 3 – Straight 8s feel

Grade 2

Part 1   Time Signature

The examiner will play a rhythmic phrase twice on the snare drum in a particular time signature appropriate to the grade (see page 3). The pulse will be given and accents placed on the first beat of the bar. The candidate will be asked to identify the time signature.

Example 1

Example 2

Example 3

Part 2   Style Recognition

The examiner will play a short piece twice on the drum kit in a particular musical style appropriate to the grade (see page 3). The candidate will be asked to identify the style.

Example 1 – $\frac{12}{8}$ feel

Example 2 – Basic $\frac{2}{4}$ March

Part 3   Identify the Changes

The examiner will play a short piece twice on the drum kit. On the second playing a change will be introduced to *either* the rhythm (rhythm change) *or* the drums/cymbals played (pattern change). The candidate will be asked to identify the type of change.

Example 1

original version

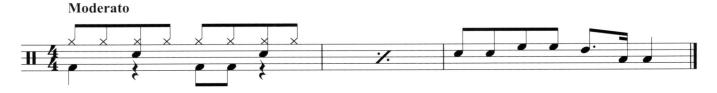

a) changed version – rhythm change

b) changed version – pattern change

Example 2

original version

a) changed version – rhythm change

b) changed version – pattern change

Example 3

original version

a) changed version – rhythm change

b) changed version – pattern change

Part 4   Playalong

The examiner will play a melody twice on the piano. On the second playing, the candidate will be asked to accompany the examiner on the drum kit using appropriate style, rhythm and fills. The style, time signature and a count-in will be given before the second playing.

Example 1 – Straight 8s feel

Example 2 – Straight 8s feel

Example 3 – Straight 8s feel

Grade 3

Part 1   Time Signature

The examiner will play a rhythmic phrase twice on the snare drum in a particular time signature appropriate to the grade (see page 3). The pulse will be given and accents placed on the first beat of the bar. The candidate will be asked to identify the time signature.

Example 1

Example 2

Example 3

Part 2   Style Recognition

The examiner will play a short piece twice on the drum kit in a particular musical style appropriate to the grade (see page 3). The candidate will be asked to identify the style.

Example 1 – Basic Rhumba

Example 2 – Indie Rock

Part 3   Identify the Changes

The candidate will be handed a copy of a short piece of music. The examiner will play this piece three times on the drum kit. On the second playing a change will be introduced to *either* the rhythm (rhythm change) *or* the drums/cymbals played (pattern change). The examiner will then play the changed version once more, after which the candidate will be asked to identify the bar in which the change occurred.

Example 1

original version

a) changed version – rhythm change

b) changed version – pattern change

Example 2

original version

a) changed version – rhythm change

b) changed version – pattern change

Example 3

original version

a) changed version – rhythm change

b) changed version – pattern change

Part 4   Playalong

The examiner will play a melody twice on the piano. On the second playing, the candidate will be asked to accompany the examiner on the drum kit using appropriate style, rhythm and fills. The style, time signature and a count-in will be given before the second playing.

Example 1 – $\frac{3}{4}$ Straight

Example 2 – $\frac{12}{8}$ feel

Example 3 – Straight 8s feel

Grade 4

Part 1   Time Signature

The examiner will play a rhythmic phrase twice on the snare drum in a particular time signature appropriate to the grade (see page 3). The pulse will be given and accents placed on the first beat of the bar. The candidate will be asked to identify the time signature.

Example 1

Example 2

Example 3

Example 4

Part 2   Style Recognition

The examiner will play a short piece twice on the drum kit in a particular musical style appropriate to the grade (see page 3). The candidate will be asked to identify the style.

Example 1 – Bossa Nova

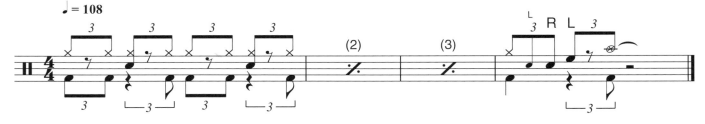

Example 2 – Shuffle

Example 3 – Show 2 feel

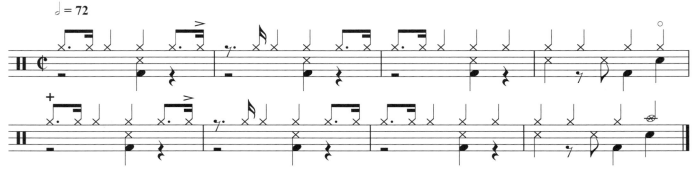

Example 4 – Reggae

Part 3　Identify the Changes

The candidate will be handed a copy of a short piece of music. The examiner will play this piece three times on the drum kit. On the second playing a change will be introduced to *either* the rhythm (rhythm change) *or* the drums/cymbals played (pattern change). The examiner will then play the changed version once more, after which the candidate will be asked to identify the bar in which the change occurred *and* the type of change.

Example 1

original version

a) changed version – rhythm change

b) changed version – pattern change

Example 2

original version

a) changed version – rhythm change

b) changed version – pattern change

Example 3

original version

a) changed version – rhythm change

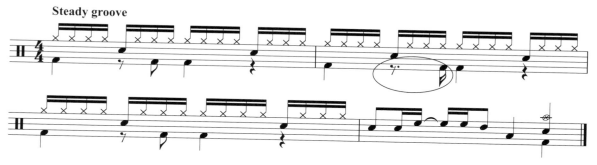

b) changed version – pattern change

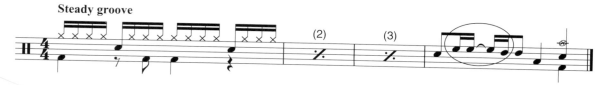

Part 4   Playalong

The examiner will play a melody twice on the piano. On the second playing, the candidate will be asked to accompany the examiner on the drum kit using appropriate style, rhythm and fills. The style, time signature and a count-in will be given before the second playing.

Example 1 – Straight 8s feel

Example 2 – Basic Latin feel

Example 3 – Bossa Nova

Grade 5

Part 1   Time Signature

The examiner will play a rhythmic phrase twice on the snare drum in a particular time signature appropriate to the grade (see page 3). The pulse will be given and accents placed on the first beat of the bar. The candidate will be asked to identify the time signature.

Example 1

Example 2

Example 3

Part 2   Style Recognition

The examiner will play a short piece twice on the drum kit in a particular musical style appropriate to the grade (see page 3). The candidate will be asked to identify the style.

Example 1 – Swing

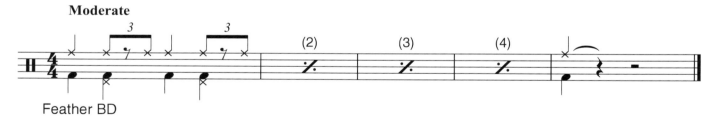

Example 2 – Jazz Waltz

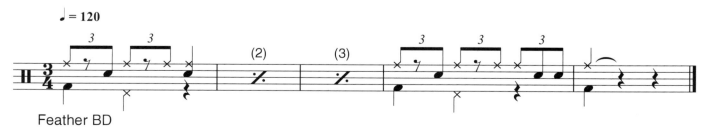

Example 3 – Tango

Example 4 – Disco

Part 3   Identify the Changes

The candidate will be handed a copy of a short piece of music. The examiner will play this piece three times on the drum kit. On the second playing, **two** separate changes will be introduced; one to the rhythm (rhythm change) *and* one to the drums/cymbals played (pattern change). The examiner will then play the changed version once more, after which the candidate will be asked to identify the bars in which the changes occurred *and* the type of change.

Example 1
original version

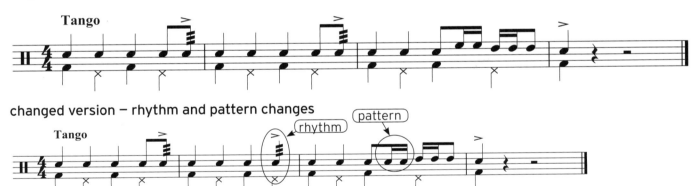

changed version – rhythm and pattern changes

Example 2
original version

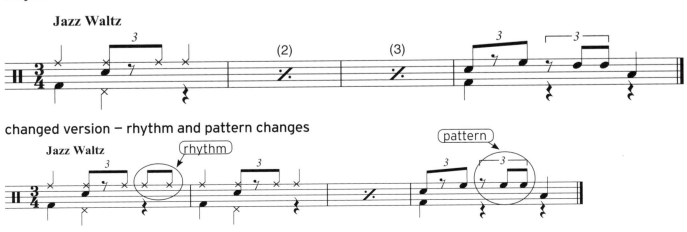

changed version – rhythm and pattern changes

Example 3

original version

changed version – rhythm and pattern changes

Part 4   Playalong

The examiner will play a melody twice on the piano. On the second playing, the candidate will be asked to accompany the examiner on the drum kit using appropriate style, rhythm and fills. The time signature and a count-in will be given before the second playing. Candidates are expected to recognise the style at this level.

Example 1 – Tango

Example 2 – Swing

Grade 6

Part 1   Time Signature

The examiner will play a rhythmic phrase twice on the snare drum in a particular time signature appropriate to the grade (see page 3). The pulse will be given and accents placed on the first beat of the bar. The candidate will be asked to identify the time signature.

Example 1

Example 2

Example 2

Part 2   Style Recognition

The examiner will play a short piece twice on the drum kit in a particular musical style appropriate to the grade (see page 3). The candidate will be asked to identify the style.

Example 1 – Funk

Example 2 – Samba

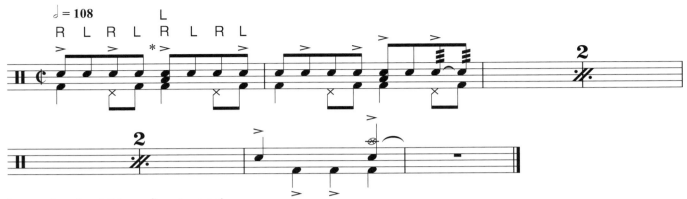

* accent on beat 3 is on floor tom only.

Example 3 – $\frac{6}{8}$ Afro Cuban

Part 3   Identify the Changes

The candidate will be handed a copy of a short piece of music. The examiner will play this piece three times on the drum kit. On the second playing, **two** changes will be introduced. The changes may be *either* a rhythm change *or* a pattern change *or* a rhythm and pattern change. The examiner will then play the changed version once more, after which the candidate will be asked to identify the bars in which the changes occurred *and* the type of change.

Example 1

original version

changed version – rhythm and pattern changes

Example 2

original version

changed version – rhythm and pattern changes

Example 3

original version

changed version – rhythm and pattern changes

Part 4   Playalong

The examiner will play a melody twice on the piano. On the second playing, the candidate will be asked to accompany the examiner on the drum kit using appropriate style, rhythm and fills. The time signature and a count-in will be given before the second playing. Candidates are expected to recognise the style at this level.

Example 1 – Jazz Waltz

Example 2 – Samba

Grade 7

Part 1   Time Signature

The examiner will play a rhythmic phrase twice on the snare drum in a particular time signature appropriate to the grade (see page 3). The pulse will be given and accents placed on the first beat of the bar. The candidate will be asked to identify the time signature.

Example 1

Example 2

Example 3

Part 2   Style Recognition

The examiner will play a short piece twice on the drum kit in a particular musical style appropriate to the grade (see page 3). The candidate will be asked to identify the style.

Example 1 – Mambo

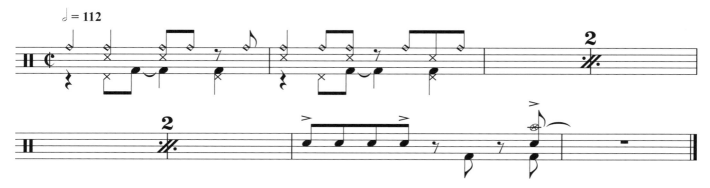

Part 3   Identify the Changes

The candidate will be handed a copy of a short piece of music. The examiner will play this piece three times on the drum kit. On the second playing, **three** changes will be introduced. The changes may be *either* a rhythm change *or* a pattern change *or* a rhythm and pattern change. The examiner will then play the changed version once more, after which the candidate will be asked to identify the bars in which the changes occurred *and* give a detailed explanation of the nature of the changes.

Example 1

original version

changed version – rhythm and pattern changes

Example 2

original version

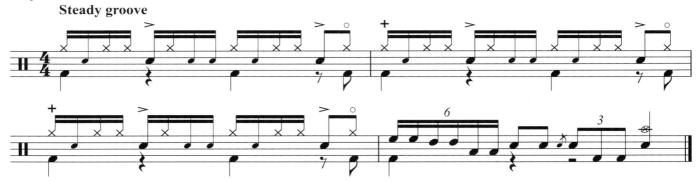

changed version – rhythm and pattern changes

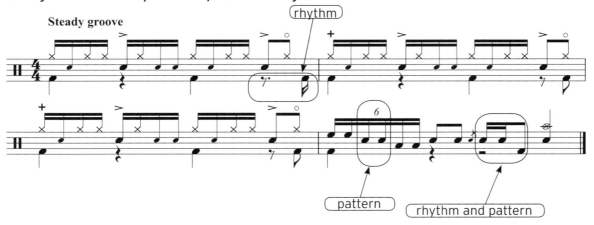

Example 3

original version

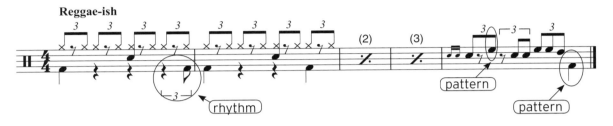

changed version – rhythm and pattern changes

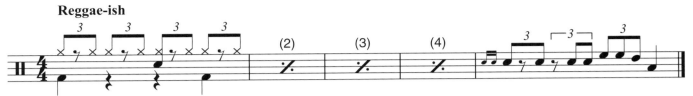

Part 4   Playalong

The examiner will play a melody twice on the piano. On the second playing, the candidate will be asked to accompany the examiner on the drum kit using appropriate style, rhythm and fills. TThe time signature and a count-in will be given before the second playing. Candidates are expected to recognise the style at this level.

Example 1 – Funk

Example 2 – $\frac{6}{8}$ Afro Cuban

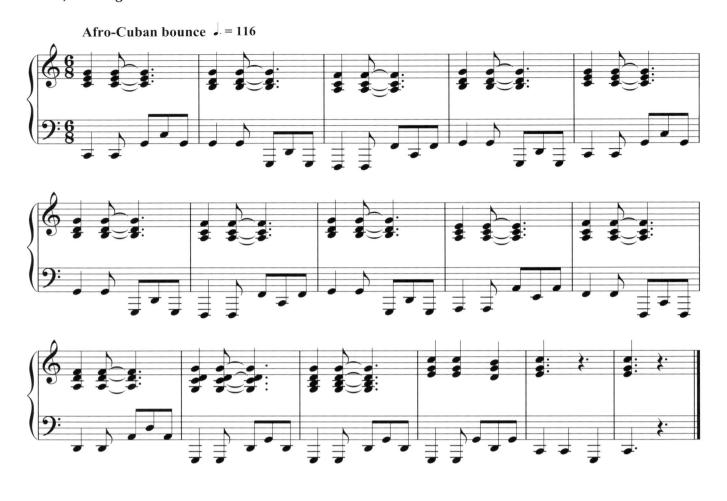

Example 3 – Straight 8s feel *or* Indie Rock

Grade 8

Part 1   Time Signature

The examiner will play a rhythmic phrase twice on the snare drum in a particular time signature appropriate to the grade (see page 3). The pulse will be given and accents placed on the first beat of the bar. The candidate will be asked to identify the time signature.

Example 1

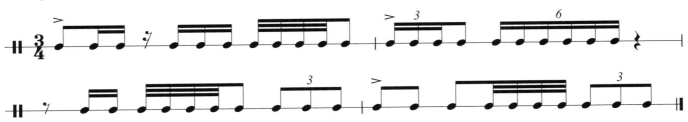

Example 2

Example 3

Example 4

Part 2   Style Recognition

The examiner will play a short piece twice on the drum kit in a particular musical style appropriate to the grade (see page 3). The candidate will be asked to identify the style.

Example 1 – New Orleans 2nd Line

Part 3   Identify the Changes

The candidate will be handed a copy of a short piece of music. The examiner will play this piece three times on the drum kit. On the second playing, **three** changes will be introduced. The changes may be *either* a rhythm change *or* a pattern change *or* a rhythm and pattern change. The examiner will then play the changed version once more, after which the candidate will be asked to identify the bars in which the changes occurred *and* give a detailed explanation of the nature of the changes.

Example 1

original version

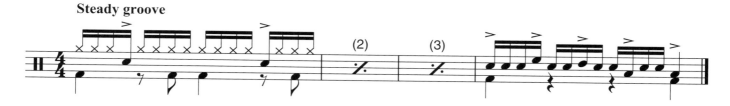

changed version – rhythm and pattern changes

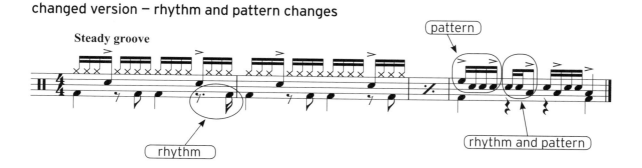

Example 2

original version

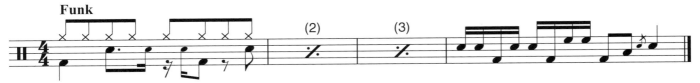

changed version – rhythm and pattern changes

Example 3

original version

changed version – rhythm and pattern changes

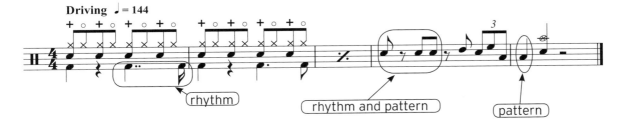

Part 4   Playalong

The examiner will play a melody twice on the piano. On the second playing, the candidate will be asked to accompany the examiner on the drum kit using appropriate style, rhythm and fills. The time signature and a count-in will be given before the second playing. Candidates are expected to recognise the style at this level.

Example 1 – Latin feel

Example 2 – Straight feel

Example 3 – Funk

Candidate's copy

Part 3 Identify the Changes

Grade 3

Example 1

Example 2

Example 3

Grade 4

Example 1

Example 2

Example 3

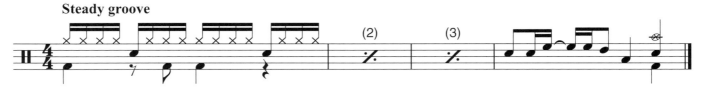

This page may be photocopied

Grade 5

Example 1

Tango

Example 2

Jazz Waltz

Example 3

Moderato

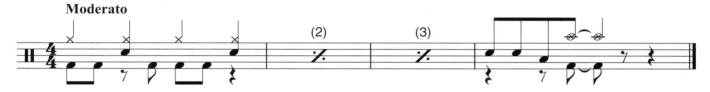

Grade 6

Example 1

Funk

Example 2

Jazz Waltz

Example 3

Steady groove

Grade 7

Example 1

Afro-Cuban groove

Example 2

Steady groove

Example 3

Reggae-ish

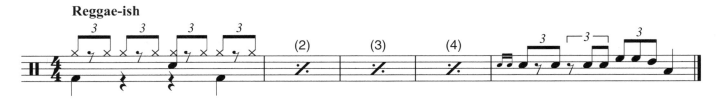

Grade 8

Example 1

Steady groove

Example 2

Funk

Example 3

Driving ♩ = 144

This page may be photocopied